Mocktails

Mocktails

Alcohol-free drinks for every occasion

Bounty Books

First published in 2010 by Bounty Books, a division of Octopus Publishing Group Limited,
Endeavour House, 189 Shaftesbury Avenue, London WC2H 8JY
www.octopusbooks.co.uk

An Hachette UK company
www.hachette.co.uk

ISBN: 978-0-753719-66-4

A catalogue record for this book is available from the British Library

Printed in China

Notes for American readers

The measure that has been used in the recipes is based on a bar measure,
which is 25 ml (1 fl oz). If preferred, a different volume can be used
providing the proportions are kept constant within a drink and suitable
adjustments are made to spoon measurements, where they occur.

Standard level spoon measurements are used in all recipes.
1 tablespoon = one 15 ml spoon
1 teaspoon = one 5 ml spoon
Imperial and metric measurements have been given in some of the recipes.
Use one set of measurements only.

UK	US
caster sugar	granulated sugar
cocktail cherries	maraschino cherries
cocktail stick	toothpick
double cream	heavy cream
drinking chocolate	presweetened cocoa powder
icing sugar	confectioners' sugar
jug	pitcher
lemon rind	lemon peel or zest
single cream	light cream
soda water	club soda

SAFETY NOTE The Department of Health advises that eggs should not be
consumed raw. This book contains recipes made with raw eggs. It is prudent
for more vulnerable people such as pregnant women and nursing mothers,
invalids, the elderly, babies and young children to avoid these recipes.

Contents

This chapter contains a wide-ranging selection of delicious drinks for large numbers of people. Choices include Tropical Treat, an unusual fresh pineapple drink with a yogurt base, the refreshing Grapefruit Mint Cooler, or the fruity Midsummer Punch.

Romanov Fizz and Bugs Bunny are among the many drinks in the chapter that will appeal as much to health-conscious adults as to children.

Iced Apple Tea and Florentine Coffee can be enjoyed at any time of the day, while more sophisticated cocktails such as Pink Tonic and Virgin Mary will appeal to those who prefer something more in the style of an alcoholic drink at cocktail hour.

This chapter includes a selection of delicious snacks and canapes to accompany your cocktails; perfect for either a party or a little individual indulgence.

Introduction

Alcohol-free drinks are becoming increasingly popular with those who are driving, those who worry about their health, those who simply prefer not to drink, and with children who want sophisticated drinks of their own. At parties it is essential to provide a range of soft drinks, so why not make your guests feel especially welcome, whether they are drinking or not, by providing a range of both alcoholic and alcohol-free cocktails. Long gone are the days when a few bottles of cola were considered sufficient for the non-drinkers.

Just because cocktails contain no alcohol doesn't mean they have to be dull and predictable. This book offers a selection of tempting drinks for any occasion, whether it is a summer garden party, a New Year's gathering or a dinner party.

By the use of unusual ingredients and exciting combinations, alcohol-free drinks can be just as appealing as those with alcohol.

When making alcohol-free drinks, use the best quality ingredients for the best results. This is especially important with fruit- and vegetable-based drinks as the quality of the fresh produce will have a great effect on the flavour of the finished drink. Choose ripe, juicy fruits, but avoid those that are over-ripe or too soft as the flavour will be affected. An electric juicer is a useful tool for those who plan to make a lot of fruit-based drinks, as it allows you to produce your own delicious juices from all sorts of fruits. Homemade juice is more flavoursome and certainly contains more nutrients than bought juices, and you will be able to make just about any of your own exciting concoctions.

One of the keys to making alcohol-free drinks seem special is in their presentation. Invest a bit of time and effort choosing the right glasses and making decorations for the drinks; they can be prepared in advance, leaving you time to relax when your guests arrive.

Many fruits lend themselves to decorating the rims of glasses. Try fixing slices of lemon, orange, lime, kiwifruit, apple or starfruit over the rim, or cut wedges of pineapple, mango, banana or melon and slide these in place. Alternatively, spear them on cocktail sticks and suspend them over the drink.

For a special occasion, consider frosting the rims of the glasses. This can be done with sugar or salt, depending on the drink. Usually the rim of the glass is dipped in beaten egg white, then in the salt or sugar, but it is possible to dip the rim in a syrup such as grenadine, then in the sugar. Glasses can also be filmed with Angostura bitters; although alcoholic, the bitters are used in such small quantities that the alcohol content is negligible.

Although most of the drinks in this book are suitable for special occasions, many are simple enough to become everyday favourites. And some of the drinks, especially those based on fruit juices, are packed with nutrients and offer a great way to provide children with their necessary vitamins.

Sugar Syrup

This may be used instead of sugar to sweeten cocktails and give them more body. It can be bought, but is simple to make. Put 4 tablespoons of caster sugar and 4 tablespoons of water in a small pan and stir over a low heat until the sugar has dissolved. Bring to the boil and boil, without stirring, for 1–2 minutes. It can be stored in a sterilized bottle in the refrigerator for up to 2 months.

Catering
for Crowds

Cool Passion

Limeade

Lemonade on the Rocks

Midsummer Punch

Bitter Sweet

Grapefruit Mint Cooler

Alcohol-free Sangria

Warbine Cooler

Clayton's Pussyfoot

Iced Mint Tea

Fruit Punch

Cranberry Crush

Tropical Treat

Nursery Fizz

Green Devil

Spiced Ginger Punch

Prohibition Punch

Cool Passion

500 ml (17 fl oz) orange
and passion fruit juice
1 litre (1¾ pints)
pineapple juice
1.5 litres (2½ pints)
lemonade
crushed ice

to decorate
blackberries
mint sprigs

Pour the two fruit juices into
a large jug. Stir well to mix.
Just before serving, stir in the
lemonade. Pour into glasses
containing crushed ice
and decorate with a blackberry
and mint sprig.

Serves 20

Limeade

6 limes
125 g (4 oz) caster sugar
750 ml (1¼ pints) boiling
   water
pinch of salt
ice cubes

to decorate
lime wedges
mint leaves

Halve the limes then squeeze
the juice into a large jug. Put
the squeezed lime halves into a
heatproof jug with the sugar and
boiling water and leave to infuse
for 15 minutes. Add the salt, give
the infusion a good stir, then
strain it into the jug with the lime
juice. Add half a dozen ice cubes,
cover and refrigerate for 2 hours
or until chilled. To serve, place
3–4 ice cubes in each glass and
pour the limeade over them.
Add a lime wedge and a mint
leaf to decorate.

Serves 8

Lemonade on the Rocks

2 lemons, roughly
chopped
2–3 tablespoons icing
sugar
600 ml (1 pint) water
soda water or mineral
water
ice cubes
lemon or lime slices, to
decorate (optional)

Put the lemons, 2 tablespoons of
the icing sugar and half the water
in a food processor and process
for a few seconds. Add the
remaining water and process
again. Taste and add more icing
sugar if required; process briefly.
Strain into 4 tumblers over ice
and top up with soda or mineral
water. Decorate with lemon
or lime slices, if liked.

Serves 4

Midsummer Punch

125 g (4 oz) sugar
300 ml (½ pint) water
300 ml (½ pint) orange
    juice
300 ml (½ pint) pineapple
    juice
600 ml (1 pint) cold weak
    tea, strained
orange, lemon, apple and
    pineapple slices
crushed ice
300 ml (½ pint) ginger ale
mint sprigs, to decorate

Put the sugar and water into a saucepan and stir over a low heat until the sugar has dissolved. Leave to cool, then pour into a large jug or bowl. Stir in the fruit juices and cold tea, then add the sliced fruit and the crushed ice. To serve, pour into tall glasses and top up with ginger ale. Decorate with mint sprigs.

Serves 8–10

Bitter Sweet

crushed ice
600 ml (1 pint) sparkling
   mineral water
8 dashes Angostura
   bitters
handful of mint leaves
lemon or lime slices,
   to decorate

Put the crushed ice into a cocktail
shaker, pour over 3 tablespoons
of the mineral water and the
bitters and add the mint leaves.
Shake until a frost forms on the
outside of the shaker. Pour into
chilled glasses, top up with the
remaining mineral water and
decorate each glass with lemon
or lime slices.

Serves 4

Grapefruit Mint Cooler

125 g (4 oz) sugar
125 ml (4 fl oz) water
handful of mint sprigs
juice of 4 large lemons
450 ml (¾ pint) grapefruit
    juice
crushed ice
250 ml (8 fl oz) soda
    water
mint sprigs, to decorate

Put the sugar and water into a heavy-based saucepan and stir over a low heat until dissolved. Leave to cool. Crush the mint leaves and stir them into the syrup. Cover and leave to stand for about 12 hours, then strain into a jug. Add the lemon and grapefruit juices to the strained syrup and stir well. Fill 6 old-fashioned glasses or tumblers with crushed ice and pour the cocktail into the glasses. Pour in the soda water and decorate with mint sprigs.

Serves 6

Alcohol-free Sangria

1 litre (1¾ pints) orange juice
sugar syrup (see page 7)
2 litres (3½ pints) red grape juice
juice of 6 lemons
juice of 6 limes
20–30 ice cubes
orange, lemon and lime slices, to decorate

Pour the orange juice and sugar syrup, to taste, into a punch bowl and stir. Add the grape, lemon and lime juices and stir thoroughly to mix. Add the ice, then float the fruit slices on top.

Serves 20

Warbine Cooler

2 dashes Angostura
    bitters
1 dash lime juice
ginger beer
lime slices, to decorate

Stir the bitters and lime juice together in a large wine glass. Top up with ginger beer and decorate with lime slices. Serve with a straw. Make to order at a party.

Serves 1

Clayton's Pussyfoot

½ measure lemon syrup
½ measure orange juice
1 measure cola
3 cracked ice cubes

This cocktail is so quick and simple to make that it can be made to order at a party, making the drivers feel as welcome as the drinkers.

Put all the ingredients into a cocktail shaker and shake well. Strain into a cocktail glass.

Serves 1

Iced Mint Tea

12 mint sprigs
1 lemon, finely chopped
1 tablespoon sugar
1.2 litres (2 pints) weak
    tea, strained
ice cubes
lemon slices, to decorate

Chop up the mint sprigs and put them into a large heatproof jug with the lemon and sugar. Pour the tea into the jug and set the mixture aside to infuse for 20–30 minutes. Strain into another jug and chill in the refrigerator until required. To serve, pour into tumblers or tall glasses filled with ice and decorate each glass with lemon slices.

Serves 4

Fruit Punch

600 ml (1 pint) orange
juice
600 ml (1 pint) apple
juice
150 ml (¼ pint) water
½ teaspoon ground
ginger
½ teaspoon mixed spice
brown sugar (optional)
1 apple, thinly sliced,
to decorate

A delicious warm, alcohol-free punch that is ideal for autumn and winter parties.

Place the orange and apple juices, water and spices in a saucepan and bring gently to the boil, adding sugar to taste if required. Simmer the mixture for 5 minutes. Pour the punch into a warmed bowl and float the apple slices on top.

Serves 6

Cranberry Crush

crushed ice
1.8 litres (3 pints)
cranberry juice
600 ml (1 pint) orange
juice
600 ml (1 pint) ginger ale
orange and lemon
wedges, to decorate

Half-fill a large punch bowl with crushed ice. Pour in the cranberry and orange juices and stir to mix. Top up with the ginger ale and decorate with orange and lemon wedges. Serve immediately.

Serves 15

Tropical Treat

900 ml (1½ pints) natural
  yogurt
1 large ripe pineapple,
  peeled and roughly
  chopped
300 ml (½ pint) sparkling
  mineral water
ice cubes
sugar syrup (see page 7)
mint sprigs, to decorate

Place the yogurt, pineapple and mineral water in a food processor and process until smooth, in batches if necessary. Put the ice cubes into a tall jug, then pour in the drink through a very fine strainer. Stir, then add sugar syrup to taste and stir again. Pour into tall glasses and decorate with mint sprigs.

Serves 4

Nursery Fizz

crushed ice
orange juice
ginger ale

to decorate
cocktail cherry
orange slice

Fill a large wine glass with crushed ice and pour in equal measures of orange juice and ginger ale. Decorate with a cocktail cherry and an orange slice speared on to a cocktail stick. Serve with a straw. Make to order at a party.

Serves 1

Green Devil

juice of 5–6 limes,
strained
1.2 litres (2 pints)
sparkling mineral
water
1 teaspoon Angostura
bitters
12 ice cubes

Combine all the ingredients,
except the ice cubes, in a jug and
stir together. Divide the ice cubes
among 4 tall glasses then pour in
the drink.

Serves 4

Spiced Ginger Punch

2 oranges
cloves, to taste
1 cm (½ inch) piece of
    fresh root ginger,
    peeled and grated
2 litres (3½ pints) ginger
    ale
10 cm (4 inches)
    cinnamon stick

Stud the oranges with the cloves, then bake them in a preheated oven at 180°C (350°F), Gas Mark 4 for about 25 minutes, until they are a rich golden colour. Cut the oranges into slices using a sharp knife then put them into a saucepan with the grated ginger, ginger ale and the cinnamon stick. Bring steadily to boiling point, but do not boil. Remove the cinnamon stick then pour the punch into heatproof glasses and serve.

Serves 12

Prohibition Punch

125 ml (4 fl oz) sugar
   syrup (see page 7)
350 ml (12 fl oz) lemon
   juice
900 ml (1½ pints) apple
   juice
ice cubes
2.5 litres (4 pints) ginger
   ale
orange slices,
   to decorate

Stir together the sugar syrup, lemon and apple juices in a large chilled jug. Add the ice cubes and pour in the ginger ale. Decorate with orange slices and serve.

Serves 25–30

Fruit and Vegetables

Anita

Brown Horny Toad

Tenderberry

Caribbean Cocktail

River Cruise

San Francisco

Banana Shake

Bugs Bunny

Romanov Fizz

Carrot Cream

Coco-oco

Tomato and Cucumber Cooler

Guavarama

Cranberry, Raspberry and
    Orange Crush

Appleade

Carib Cream

Frosty Lime

Parson's Special

Apple Eye

Peach, Pear and Raspberry
    Crush

Anita

3 ice cubes
1 measure orange juice
1 measure lemon juice
3 dashes Angostura
    bitters
soda water

to decorate
lemon slice
orange slice

Put the ice cubes into a cocktail shaker with the orange and lemon juices and bitters and shake well. Strain into a tumbler and top up with soda water. Decorate with lemon and orange slices.

Serves 1

Brown Horny Toad

4–5 crushed ice cubes
2 measures pineapple
    juice
2 measures orange juice
1 measure lemon juice
1 tablespoon grenadine
1 teaspoon sugar syrup
    (see page 7)
pinch of ground cinnamon
pinch of ground cloves

to decorate
orange slice
lemon slice

Put the ice cubes into a cocktail shaker. Pour in the pineapple, orange and lemon juices, and the grenadine and add the sugar syrup and spices. Shake until a frost forms on the outside of the shaker. Strain into a highball glass and decorate with orange and lemon slices.

Serves 1

Tenderberry

6–8 strawberries
1 measure grenadine
1 measure double cream
crushed ice
1 measure ginger ale
ground ginger
strawberry, to decorate
    (optional)

Place the strawberries, grenadine and cream in a food processor with some crushed ice and process for 30 seconds. Pour into a glass. Add the ginger ale and stir. Sprinkle a little ground ginger on top and decorate with a strawberry, if liked.

Serves 1

Caribbean Cocktail

1 mango, peeled and
    stoned
1 banana
juice of 1 large orange
1 dash lime juice
8–10 ice cubes
lime slices, to decorate

Put the mango, banana, orange and lime juices in a food processor and process until smooth. Put the ice into 2 highball glasses and pour the cocktail over it. Decorate with lime slices.

Serves 2

River Cruise

500 g (1 lb) cantaloupe
    melon flesh
grated rind and juice of
    2 lemons
2 tablespoons sugar
600 ml (1 pint) chilled
    soda water

Remove and discard any melon seeds. Put the flesh into a food processor and process to a smooth purée. Scrape the purée into a large jug. Put the lemon rind and juice into a small saucepan with the sugar and stir over a low heat until the sugar has dissolved. Strain the lemon mixture into the melon purée and mix well. Chill in the refrigerator. Stir in the chilled soda water just before serving.

Serves 4–6

San Francisco

3 ice cubes
1 measure orange juice
1 measure lemon juice
1 measure pineapple
   juice
1 measure grapefruit
   juice
2 dashes grenadine
1 egg white
soda water

to decorate
lemon slice
lime slice
cocktail cherry
orange spiral

Put the ice cubes into a cocktail shaker and pour in the orange, lemon, pineapple and grapefruit juices, grenadine and egg white. Shake well then strain into a large goblet. Top up with soda water and decorate with the lemon and lime slices, a cocktail cherry on a cocktail stick and an orange spiral. Serve with a straw.

Serves 1

Banana Shake

1 ripe banana, chopped
juice of 1 orange
1 teaspoon honey
300 ml (½ pint) full-fat
    milk
8 ice cubes
ground cinnamon

Place the banana, orange juice, honey and milk in a food processor and process until smooth. Pour over ice into 2 tall glasses and sprinkle with cinnamon.

Serves 2

Bugs Bunny

50 ml (2 fl oz) carrot juice
50 ml (2 fl oz) orange
    juice
4–6 ice cubes
1 dash Tabasco sauce
1 celery stick, to
    decorate

Pour the carrot and orange juices into a tumbler over ice, add a dash of Tabasco and decorate with a celery stick.

Serves 1

Romanov Fizz

8–10 ripe strawberries,
hulled
125 ml (4 fl oz) orange
juice
2 ice cubes
125 ml (4 fl oz) soda
water

Put the strawberries and orange juice into a food processor and process until smooth. Place 1 ice cube in each of 2 sour glasses or wine glasses and add the strawberry liquid. Pour the soda water into the food processor, process briefly and use to top up the glasses. Stir briskly, and serve.

Serves 2

Carrot Cream

250 ml (8 fl oz) carrot
    juice
300 ml (½ pint) single
    cream
4 egg yolks
125 ml (4 fl oz) orange
    juice
20 ice cubes
orange slices, to
    decorate

Put the carrot juice, cream, egg yolks and orange juice into a cocktail shaker and shake well. Divide the ice cubes among 4 tall glasses and pour the carrot drink on top. Decorate with orange slices and serve immediately. Serve with straws.

Serves 4

Coco-oco

crushed ice
4 teaspoons creamed
   coconut or coconut
   syrup
2 teaspoons lemon juice
1 teaspoon maraschino
   syrup
100 ml (3½ fl oz) full-fat
   milk
4 dashes Angostura
   bitters

to decorate
pineapple leaf
pineapple wedge
cocktail cherry

Put the ice into a food processor
and add the creamed coconut or
coconut syrup, lemon juice,
maraschino syrup, milk and
bitters. Process for a few
seconds. Pour into a tall glass
and decorate with a pineapple
leaf, a pineapple wedge and a
cocktail cherry. Serve with
a straw.

Serves 1

fruit and vegetables

51

Tomato and Cucumber Cooler

crushed ice
150 ml (¼ pint) tomato
    juice
25 g (1 oz) cucumber,
    peeled
2 dashes lemon juice
2 dashes Worcestershire
    sauce
salt and pepper
cucumber slice, to
    decorate

Put a little crushed ice into a food
processor. Add the tomato juice,
cucumber, lemon juice,
Worcestershire sauce and salt
and pepper to taste and process
well. Pour the drink into a
cocktail glass and decorate with a
cucumber slice.

Serves 1

Guavarama

crushed ice
200 ml (7 fl oz) guava
    juice
2 teaspoons lime juice
4 teaspoons blackcurrant
    syrup
5 dashes rum essence
melon slice, to decorate

Put some crushed ice into a food
processor and add the guava
juice, lime juice, blackcurrant
syrup and rum essence. Process
thoroughly then strain into a
chilled cocktail glass and
decorate with a melon slice.

Serves 1

Cranberry, Raspberry and Orange Crush

200 ml (7 fl oz) cranberry
    juice
100 ml (3½ fl oz) orange
    juice
250 ml (8 oz) raspberries
3 scoops orange sorbet,
    plus extra to decorate
sugar syrup (see page 7)
    (optional)

Put the cranberry juice, orange juice, raspberries and sorbet into a food processor and process until frothy. Taste and add sugar syrup, if required. Serve in cocktail glasses, each with an extra scoop of sorbet.

Serves 2–3

Appleade

2 large dessert apples
600 ml (1 pint) boiling
    water
½ teaspoon sugar
ice cubes
apple slices, to decorate

Chop the apples and place in a bowl. Pour the boiling water over the apples and add the sugar. Leave to stand for 10 minutes, then strain into a jug and allow to cool. Pour over ice cubes in tall glasses and decorate with apple slices. Serve with straws.

Serves 3

Carib Cream

1 small banana, chopped
1 measure lemon juice
1 measure full-fat milk
crushed ice
1 teaspoon finely
    chopped walnuts

Place the banana, lemon juice
and milk in a food processor with
some crushed ice and process on
maximum speed until smooth.
Pour into a cocktail glass and
sprinkle the chopped walnuts
on top just before serving.

Serves 1

fruit and vegetables

57

Frosty Lime

1 scoop lime sorbet
1 measure grapefruit
    juice
4 teaspoons mint syrup

to decorate
mint strips
lemon slices

Put the sorbet, grapefruit juice
and syrup into a food processor
and process on high speed for
about 30 seconds. Strain into a
Champagne glass and decorate
with mint strips and lemon slices.

Serves 1

Parson's Special

4 dashes grenadine
120 ml (4 fl oz) orange
   juice
1 egg yolk
3 ice cubes

Put all the ingredients into a
cocktail shaker and shake well.
Stain into a tumbler.

Serves 1

Apple Eye

2 measures apple juice
½ measure blackcurrant
    syrup
1 measure double cream
crushed ice
ground cinnamon
apple slices, to decorate

Place the apple juice,
blackcurrant syrup and cream
in a food processor with
some crushed ice. Process on
maximum speed for 30 seconds.
Pour into a cocktail glass and
sprinkle a little cinnamon on top.
Decorate with apple slices.

Serves 1

Peach, Pear and Raspberry Crush

1 ripe peach, skinned,
   stoned and chopped
1 ripe pear, peeled, cored
   and chopped
125 g (4 oz) raspberries
200 ml (7 fl oz) peach
   juice
crushed ice
pear slices, to decorate

Put the peach, pear, raspberries and peach juice into a food processor with some ice and process until smooth. Serve in cocktail glasses and decorate with pear slices.

Serves 2–3

Round the Clock

Café Astoria

Chocolate Shake

Egg Nog

Tutti Frutti Verbena Cocktail

Florentine Coffee

Iced Apple Tea

Catherine Blossom

Limey

Virgin Colada

St Clements

Jersey Lily

Grenadine Soda

Pink Tonic

Shirley Temple

Honeymoon

Cinderella

Keep Sober

Virgin Mary

Dandy

Orange and Papaya Fizz

Nairobi Night

Café Astoria

1½ measures coffee
    essence
2 measures full-fat milk
1 measure pineapple
    juice
½ measure lemon juice
3 ice cubes, crushed
chocolate shavings, to
    decorate

**A great drink to start the
day, or to end a party in
the early hours.**

Place the coffee essence, milk,
pineapple juice and lemon juice
in a food processor with the ice
and process on maximum speed
for 30 seconds. Pour into a
cocktail glass and sprinkle the
chocolate shavings on top just
before serving.

Serves 1

Chocolate Shake

2 measures chocolate
  syrup
2 scoops chocolate ice
  cream
1 scoop vanilla ice cream
250 ml (8 fl oz) full-fat
  milk
whipped cream, to
  decorate (optional)

Pour all of the ingredients into
a food processor. Process well
until the desired thickness is
reached. Pour into a tall glass.
Decorate with whipped cream, if
liked, and serve with a straw.

Serves 1

Egg Nog

1 egg
sugar syrup (see page 7)
250 ml (8 fl oz) full-fat
    milk
cracked ice
grated nutmeg, to
    decorate

Combine the egg, sugar syrup to
taste, milk and ice in a cocktail
shaker and shake well. Strain into
a large goblet and sprinkle with
grated nutmeg.

Serves 1

Tutti Frutti Verbena Cocktail

3 sachets verbena tea
600 ml (1 pint) boiling
     water
juice of 2 oranges
juice of 2 lemons
150 ml (¼ pint) apricot
     juice
150 ml (¼ pint) pineapple
     juice
ice cubes

Put the sachets of verbena tea into a heatproof jug, pour over the boiling water and leave to infuse. When the tea is cold, remove the sachets from the jug. Pour the tea into another jug and add the juice from the oranges and lemons, the apricot juice, pineapple juice and a few ice cubes.

Serves 4–6

Variation

Try different flavours of fruit tea, such as elderflower, rosehip or cranberry in place of the verbena tea.

Florentine Coffee

espresso coffee
1 drop almond essence
1 sugar cube (optional)

Pour the coffee into a warmed cup or heatproof glass. Add the almond essence and sugar, if using, and stir.

Serves 1

Iced Apple Tea

¾ pint chilled weak tea
450 ml (¾ pint) apple
    juice
juice of 1 lemon
1 teaspoon sugar
    (optional)
ice cubes

to decorate
lemon slices
orange slices
mint sprigs

Mix the tea with the apple juice,
lemon juice and sugar, if using.
Add plenty of ice and decorate
with the lemon and orange
slices and mint sprigs. Serve
in tumblers or tea glasses.

Serves 6–8

Catherine Blossom

200 ml (7 fl oz) orange
  juice
2 teaspoons maple syrup
2 scoops orange sorbet
soda water

Put the orange juice, maple syrup and orange sorbet into a food processor and process for 15 seconds. Pour into a tall glass and top up with soda water.

Serves 1

Limey

1 measure lime juice
½ measure lemon juice
½ egg white
3 cracked ice cubes
cocktail cherry, to
decorate

**This makes a refreshing
late afternoon drink for
a warm summer's day.**

Put the lime and lemon juces,
egg white and ice cubes into a
cocktail shaker and shake well.
Strain into a cocktail glass and
decorate with a cocktail cherry
on a cocktail stick.

Serves 1

Virgin Colada

1 measure coconut
    cream
2 measures pineapple
    juice
crushed ice
pineapple wedge, to
    decorate

Place the coconut cream,
pineapple juice and crushed ice
into a food processor and
process, or shake in a cocktail
shaker. Pour into a tall glass and
decorate with a pineapple
wedge. Serve with a straw.

Serves 1

St Clements

2 measures orange juice
2 measures bitter lemon
4 ice cubes
orange slice, to decorate

Pour the orange juice and bitter lemon over ice in a tumbler, stir together and decorate with the orange slice.

Serves 1

Jersey Lily

150 ml (¼ pint) sparkling apple juice
2 dashes Angostura bitters
¼ teaspoon caster sugar
ice cubes
cocktail cherry, to decorate

Put the apple juice, bitters, sugar and ice cubes in a cocktail shaker. Shake well, then strain into a wine glass. Decorate with a cocktail cherry.

Serves 1

Variation

Sparkling grape juice, either red or white, makes a refreshing substitute for the apple juice.

Grenadine Soda

1 scoop orange sorbet
1 scoop raspberry sorbet
3 tablespoons grenadine
juice of 1 lime
2 scoops vanilla ice
    cream
250 ml (8 fl oz) soda
    water

to decorate
1 finely chopped orange
    slice
raspberries

Put the sorbets, grenadine and lime juice into a food processor and process until slushy. Pour into glasses and put the vanilla ice cream on top. Top up with soda water. Stir gently, and decorate with the fruit. Serve with straws.

Serves 2

Pink Tonic

2–3 dashes Angostura
   bitters
4–6 ice cubes
250 ml (8 fl oz) tonic
   water
lime wedge, to decorate

Drop the bitters over ice in a
tumbler, add the tonic water
and stir well. Decorate with a
lime wedge.

Serves 1

Shirley Temple

4–5 ice cubes
1 dash grenadine
ginger ale
2 cocktail cherries,
    to decorate

Put the ice cubes in a glass. Add
the grenadine and top up with
the ginger ale. Decorate with 2
cherries on a cocktail stick.

Serves 1

Honeymoon

crushed ice
1 measure maple syrup
  or clear honey
4 teaspoons lime juice
1 measure orange juice
1 measure apple juice
cocktail cherry,
  to decorate

Put some crushed ice into a cocktail shaker and add the maple syrup or honey, lime juice, orange juice and apple juice. Shake well then strain into a chilled cocktail glass. Decorate with a cherry on a cocktail stick.

Serves 1

Cinderella

1 measure lemon juice
1 measure pineapple
    juice
1 measure orange juice
1 dash grenadine
3 ice cubes, cracked
soda water
pineapple slices,
    to decorate

Put the lemon, pineapple and
orange juices, grenadine and ice
into a cocktail shaker and shake
well. Strain into a tall tumbler.
Top up with soda water and
decorate with pineapple slices.
Serve with a straw.

Serves 1

Keep Sober

½ measure grenadine
½ measure lemon syrup
3 measures tonic water
soda water
ice cubes (optional)

Put the grenadine, lemon syrup and tonic water in a tumbler and stir together. Top up with soda water and add ice cubes, if liked.

Serves 1

Variation

For a tangier drink, replace the grenadine with lime syrup and decorate the drink with lime slices.

Virgin Mary

4 measures tomato juice
ice cubes
½ measure lemon juice
2 dashes Worcestershire
    sauce
1 dash Tabasco sauce
celery stick, to decorate

Pour the tomato juice into a glass
over ice cubes, add the lemon
juice and Worcestershire and
Tabasco sauces and stir well.
Serve with a celery stick.

Serves 1

Variation

For special occasions,
dip the rim of the glass
into beaten egg white,
then into celery salt
for an attractive and
tasty frosting.

Dandy

3 measures apple juice
1 measure strawberry
    syrup
1 measure lime juice
10 blackberries

to decorate
blackberry
mint sprig

Put the apple juice, strawberry syrup, lime juice and blackberries in a food processor with some cracked ice and process until smooth. Pour into a tall glass. Decorate with a blackberry and a mint sprig.

Serves 1

Orange and Papaya Fizz

1 papaya, peeled,
     quartered and
     deseeded
250 ml (8 fl oz) orange
     juice
4–6 ice cubes
sparkling mineral water
mint sprigs, to decorate

Place the papaya and orange juice
in a food processor and process
for about 30 seconds, or until
smooth. Put 2–3 ice cubes into 2
tall glasses, pour in the drink and
top up with the sparkling mineral
water. Stir and serve, decorated
with mint sprigs.

Serves 2

Nairobi Night

450 ml (¾ pint) freshly
      made coffee
caster sugar
4 tablespoons single
      cream
150 ml (¼ pint) vanilla ice
      cream
4 ice cubes
drinking chocolate
      powder, to decorate

Pour the coffee into a bowl and
stir in sugar to taste. Set aside to
cool. Whisk together the cream
and ice cream, then beat into the
coffee. Continue beating until
smooth and frothy. Pour into a
jug and chill in the refrigerator
for 1 hour, stirring occasionally.
To serve, pour into 2 large
goblets and float the ice cubes
on top. Sprinkle with drinking
chocolate powder to decorate.

Serves 2

Finger food

Chilli Chips
Crispy Ricotta Parcels
Root Vegetable Crisps
Savoury Samosas
Toasted Chilli Cashews
Polenta Triangles
Spiced Chicken Wings
Prawns with Plum Sauce

Chilli Chips

4 large baking potatoes
4–6 tablespoons olive oil
½ teaspoon salt
1–2 teaspoons chilli
    powder, to taste
salad leaves, to garnish
soured cream or
    mayonnaise, to serve

Use as little or as much chilli powder as you like, to coat these oven-roasted potato chips.

Serves: 4–6
Preparation time: 5 minutes
Cooking time: about 1 hour
Oven temperature: 220°C/425°F/Gas Mark 7

1 Cut each potato into 8 wedges and place in a large bowl. Add the oil, salt and chilli powder and toss until evenly coated.

2 Transfer the potatoes to a baking sheet and roast in a preheated oven at 220°C/425°F/Gas Mark 7 for 15 minutes. Turn them over and cook for a further 15 minutes. Turn once more and cook for a final 25–30 minutes until crisp and golden.

3 Cool slightly and serve with soured cream or mayonnaise, garnished with salad leaves.

Crispy Ricotta Parcels

250 g/8 oz ricotta cheese
125 g/4 oz frozen
  spinach, chopped and
  squeezed dry
¼ teaspoon ground
  nutmeg
8 sheets filo pastry
75 g/3 oz butter, melted
pepper
cress, to garnish
  (optional)

Makes: 24
Preparation time: 30 minutes
Cooking time: 8–10 minutes
Oven temperature: 220°C/425°F/Gas Mark 7

1 Place the ricotta cheese in a bowl with the spinach and nutmeg and add pepper to taste. Mix well.

2 Put the sheets of filo pastry on a plate and cover with a damp tea towel. Working with one sheet of pastry at a time, cut each sheet into three equal strips and brush well with butter. Place a teaspoon of the cheese mixture at one end of each strip. Fold over diagonally to enclose the filling in a triangle of pastry and continue folding to make a neat three-cornered parcel.

3 Brush the parcel with more butter and place on a baking sheet. Repeat with the remaining filling, pastry and butter, to make a total of
24 small parcels.

4 Bake the parcels in a preheated oven at 220°C/425°F/Gas Mark 7 for 8–10 minutes until golden brown. Serve hot garnished with cress, if liked.

Root Vegetable crisps

2 beetroots
1 large potato
1 small sweet potato
2 carrots
2 parsnips
vegetable oil, for deep-
    frying
sea salt
cayenne pepper
    (optional)

These crisps are easy to make at home, which means, of course, that you can use your favourite root vegetables.

Serves: **4–6**
Preparation time: 10 minutes
Cooking time: 8–10 minutes

1 Slice the vegetables into fine wafers using a potato peeler or mandoline, keeping them in separate batches. (It is best to cut the carrots and parsnips lengthways.)

2 Heat 5 cm/2 inches of vegetable oil in a deep saucepan until it reaches 180–190°C/350–375°F, or until a cube of bread browns in 30 seconds. Pat the vegetables dry on kitchen paper.

3 Again, keeping the vegetables separate, deep-fry them in batches for 30 seconds to 1½ minutes, until crisp and golden. Drain on kitchen paper and leave to cool on a wire rack.

4 Put the crisps into a large bowl and sprinkle with sea salt and a little cayenne, if using.

Savoury Samosas

6 sheets filo pastry
oil, for deep-frying
FILLING ONE
250 g/8 oz new
   potatoes, cooked
   and cubed
50 g/2 oz young spinach,
   cooked
1 spring onion, finely
   sliced
FILLING TWO
175 g/6 oz cooked
   chicken, diced
1 leek, sliced and
   softened
salt and pepper

Makes: **about 16**
Preparation time: 25 minutes
Cooking time: 10 minutes

1 Stir together the ingredients for the two fillings and season well to taste.

2 Lay the filo sheets on a work surface and cut them into 10 cm/4 inch wide strips. Spoon a little of the filling in the corner of each strip and fold the pastry over to form a triangle, then do this twice more. Seal with a little water, pressing well together. Trim the pastry and continue making samosas, using both fillings.

3 Heat the oil in a deep saucepan and cook the samosas, in batches, for 2–3 minutes each. Drain on kitchen paper.

4 Serve the samosas warm with the relish.

Toasted Chilli Cashews

1 tablespoon
  groundnut oil
1 garlic clove, finely
  chopped
250 g/8 oz roasted
  cashews
¼ teaspoon crushed dried
  chillies
1 spring onion, finely
  chopped
2 small fresh chillies
  (different colours),
  finely chopped
salt

Makes: **about 250g/8 oz**
Preparation time: 2 minutes
Cooking time: 2 minutes

1 Heat the oil in a wok and fry the garlic
until golden brown. Remove and discard.

2 Add the cashews to the oil and sprinkle
the crushed dried chillies over them. Stir-fry
for 1 minute, then add the spring onion,
chopped fresh chillies and salt to taste.
Serve warm.

Polenta Triangles

900 ml/1½ pints water
15 g/½ oz butter
½ teaspoon sea salt
75 g/3 oz quick
  cooking polenta
15 g/½ oz Parmesan
  cheese, grated
175 g/6 oz mozzarella
  cheese
18 large basil leaves
4 tablespoons
  seasoned flour
2 eggs, beaten
50 g/2 oz dried white
  breadcrumbs
vegetable oil, for deep-
  frying
pepper

These triangles of set polenta are
sandwiched together with mozzarella and
coated in bread-crumbs, then deep-fried
until crisp.

Makes: 18
Preparation time: 10 minutes, plus setting
  and chilling
Cooking time: 10 minutes, plus 1–2 minutes
  per batch

1 Grease a 20 x 30 cm/8 x 12 inch tin. Bring
the water to a rolling boil, add the butter and
salt and then gradually whisk in the polenta in
a steady stream. Simmer over a low heat for
5–6 minutes, stirring constantly until the
mixture comes away from the sides of the
pan. Stir in the Parmesan, season with pepper
and pour into the prepared tin. Smooth the
surface and set aside to cool.

2 Turn out the set polenta and trim to form
two 15 cm/6 inch squares. Cut each into nine 5
cm/2 inch squares and then cut each square in
half diagonally, to make 36 triangles in all.

3 Cut the mozzarella into thin slices and then
into triangles, the same size as the polenta.

4 Place a triangular slice of mozzarella over half the polenta triangles, top with a basil leaf and a second piece of polenta. Dip the polenta sandwiches in the seasoned flour, then into the beaten egg and finally into the breadcrumbs to coat well. Chill for 1 hour.

5 Heat 5 cm/2 inches vegetable oil in a deep saucepan until it reaches 180–190°C/350–375°F, or until a cube of bread browns in 30 seconds.

6 Deep-fry the triangles in batches for 1–2 minutes until crisp and golden. Drain on kitchen paper and keep warm in a hot oven while frying the rest. Serve hot.

Spiced Chicken Wings

8 large chicken wings
flat leaf parsley sprig, to
  garnish
lime wedges, to serve
MARINADE
1 garlic clove
5 cm/2 inch piece of
  fresh root ginger,
  peeled and chopped
juice and finely grated
  rind of 2 limes
2 tablespoons light soy
  sauce
2 tablespoons groundnut
  oil
2 teaspoons ground
  cinnamon
1 teaspoon ground
  turmeric
2 tablespoons clear
  honey
salt
YELLOW PEPPER DIP
2 yellow peppers
2 tablespoons plain
  yogurt
1 tablespoon dark soy
  sauce
1 tablespoon chopped
  coriander
pepper

Serves: **4**
Preparation time: 10 minutes,
  plus marinating
Cooking time: 18–20 minutes

1 Place the marinade ingredients in a blender or food processor and blend until smooth.

2 Place the chicken in a bowl and pour over the marinade. Toss, cover and leave to marinate for 1–2 hours.

3 To make the dip, put the peppers under a preheated grill for 10 minutes, turning occasionally until they are charred and blistered. Put them into a plastic bag until cool, then peel off the skin and remove the seeds and white membrane. Put the flesh into a food processor or blender with the yogurt and blend until smooth. Pour into a bowl, season with soy sauce and pepper to taste and stir in the coriander. Cover and chill until needed.

4 Remove the chicken from the marinade and cook under a preheated grill or on a barbecue grill for 4–5 minutes on each side, basting with the remaining marinade. Garnish with a flat leaf parsley sprig, then serve with the dip and some lime wedges.

Prawns with Plum Sauce

finger food

4 tablespoons Chinese
  plum sauce
150 ml/¼ pint garlic
  mayonnaise
16 cooked tiger prawns,
  shelled
spring onion curls, to
  garnish

Serves: **8**
Preparation time: 10 minutes

1 Stir together the plum sauce and mayonnaise until evenly coloured and smooth. Turn into a serving bowl.

2 Serve the dip with the prawns and spring onion curls.

INDEX

NEW PHOTOGRAPHY
by William Reavell
Cocktails styled by Andrew
Fitz-Maurice at High Holborn,
95–96 High Holborn, London
WC1V 6LF

**ACKNOWLEDGEMENTS IN
SOURCE ORDER**

**Octopus Publishing Group
Limited**/ Jean Cazals 59, 71,
73, 102, 104, 106/ Neil
Mersh 19, 33, 43, 49, 81/
Peter Myers 6–7 background,
15, 91/ Sandra Lane 5, 8, 25,
27, 78, 98/ William Reavell
front cover, back cover, 2, 3,
11, 13, 21, 23, 30, 34, 39, 40,
47, 51, 53, 55, 63, 64, 68, 77,
83, 85, 87, 93, 95, 100, 101,
108, 110/ Ian Wallace 60